Copyright Notice

Strolling Around Lille by Irene Reid

ISBN: 9781652705864

Book Cover

Photo by Irene Reid

Enhanced by Prisma Photo Editor

Get Ready

La Braderie
When choosing the date for your visit, be aware that if you visit on the first weekend in September, you won't get much sightseeing done as that is when Lille is taken over by La Braderie, essentially a massive flea market with hundreds and hundreds of stalls, that centres on the Grand Place but spreads all over the Old Town.

La Braderie started long ago in medieval times. The well-off linen merchants gave permission to their servants to sell any unwanted garments and cloths to earn some extra cash. The market got bigger and bigger, until today when every street in central Lille hosts a multitude of stalls. Traditionally everyone indulges in that famous Flemish dish, moules-frites, while searching for a bargain. The restaurants selling moules compete with each other to see who can build the biggest mound of empty mussel shells.

City Pass
The city pass gives you free access to many of the sights on the walk, free public transport, and also an hour long bus tour around the city. You can buy it at the tourist office in Place Rihour or online at

http://en.lilletourism.com/city-pass.html

Passport
The Museum of Fine Arts in Lille is a must see – full of interesting paintings and statues.

The ticket also gets you a Visioguide. However, you must take your passport with you for identification before you will be issued with one, so remember to take it with you when you tackle Walk 1. Alternatively you could download the App onto your mobile before you go – look for the PBA Lille App.

The Opera

Lille has a beautiful opera house. If you would like to check what is on when you are in town, try this link.

http://www.opera-lille.fr/en/calendar/

Potted History

Lille is now of course part of France. It lies in one of the World's most fought over pieces of land and has changed hands many times.

The earliest inhabitants that we can identify were a Belgian tribe called the Nervii. They were in residence two thousand years ago when Julius Caesar marched in to "Veni, Vidi, Vici". However he found it harder to Vici than expected. Caesar himself declared that the Nervii were the most warlike of the Belgic tribes, and that the Belgic tribes were the bravest in Gaul. They were finally defeated however and became part of the Roman Empire.

Interestingly, artefacts have been found near the Antonine Wall in Scotland, with inscriptions telling us that the owners were the Sixth Cohort of Nervii. So Caesar put their warlike character to good use, keeping the Scots at bay.

After the Romans the Franks arrived. The name Lille is thought to come from the L'Isle, which was a castle built about 640 AD by a Frankish lord. It was called The Island because it was surrounded by marshy land fed by the river Deule.

The marshes weren't navigable, so Lille grew as its citizens transported goods across the marshland to rejoin the Deule on the other side of the marsh. As time passed more and more of the marsh was tamed, and canals were channelled between the outcrops of buildings. You will see some proof of that watery beginning on the walks. The canals have long been covered over, but here and there you can still find some evidence of their existence.

Lille stayed in Flemish hands until the middle ages, but was then fought over and ruled many times by France, Flanders, Spain, and Holland. It finally became French in 1667 when Louis XIV laid siege and conquered it.

In 1672, a musketeer called D'Artagnan was appointed governor of Lille, but was killed one year later in the Battle of Maastricht. He was the inspiration of Dumas's novel "The Three Musketeers".

Life was never quiet in Lille even after it became French. The Dutch marched in and held it from 1708-1713 until the French kicked them out again. The Austrians tried to conquer it by laying siege with 30,000 soldiers, but for once Lille managed to hold them off.

The Germans arrived in 1914 and 1940 and occupied Lille until forced out by the allies. Since then it's been quiet – apart from the arrival of the Eurostar which put Lille on the tourist trail.

The Napoleons

There were actually 3 Napoleons and they are mentioned at various points in the walk. So just to make it clear who was who:

Napoleon I – He was the famous one who supposedly said "Not tonight Josephine". He conquered and fought with a large part of Europe but was defeated at Waterloo by the Duke of Wellington. He died on the island of Saint Helena as a prisoner.

Napoleon II – He was the son of Napoleon I. He tried to become emperor when his father was defeated but only managed to hold on to power for one week.

Napoleon III - He was the nephew of Napoleon I. France was in turmoil and the monarchy was overthrown in the revolution. Napoleon stood for election in the national assembly and won many titles and was soon in power as president. He was actually a popular and successful ruler.

The Walks

There are two walks to help you explore Lille.

If you have limited time, tackle Walk 2 as it takes you round the old town which is the prettiest and most interesting part of Lille.

Walk 1 – Lille Centre and South (3.8km)

This walk takes you round the Grand Place and then south to visit the Palais des Beaux-Arts and the Town Hall. You return to the centre via the Lille Metro.

Walk 2 – Lille Old Town (2.7km or 4km)

This walk starts at the old city wall which lies northeast of the Grand Place. It then takes you through the old town before returning you to the Grand Place.

Getting Started

If you are arriving for the day by train, you will come into either the Eurostar terminal or Flanders Station.

If you want to start exploring straight away, use the instructions below to get to the start of Walk 1 or Walk 2.

Getting to Start of Walk 1

From the Eurostar

Exit the Eurostar building by the main door and you will be on a wide concrete square. You will see a large colourful floral statue called the Tulips of Shangri-La.

The pathway down into old Lille starts behind this statue and runs alongside the busy main road, Avenue le Corbusier, which is lined with flags.

Walk past the rather ugly shopping arcades on your left and you will reach the front of Flanders Station.

Continue From Flanders Station below...

From Flanders Station

With Flanders station behind you, carefully cross the busy road in front of you to reach Rue Faidherbe.

Walk straight down Rue Faidherbe to reach Place du Theatre. To reach the Grand Place and the start of Walk 1, turn left along Rue des Manneliers.

Getting to Start of Walk 2

From the Eurostar

Exit the Eurostar building by the main door and you will be on a wide concrete square. You will see a large colourful floral statue called the Tulips of Shangri-La. The pathway down into old Lille starts behind this statue and runs alongside the busy main road, Avenue le Corbusier, which is lined with flags.

Walk past the **first** rather ugly shopping arcade on your left. Then turn right along Rue des Cannoniers.

Continue from Rue des Cannoniers below...

From Flanders Station

With Flanders station behind you, turn right to walk up busy Avenue le Corbusier. Pass Rue des Buisses on your left. Take the next left into Rue des Canonniers.

Continue from Rue des Cannoniers below...

Rue des Cannoniers

You will pass a large modern orange building on your right and Rue du Vieux Faubourg on your left.

Walk past the orange building and you will find little Place Saint-Hubert just beyond it on your right.

Walk straight ahead to reach the end of the square where you can start Walk 2.

The Maps

There are maps sprinkled all through the walks to help you find your way. If you need to check where you are at any point during a walk, always flip back to find the map you need

To help you follow the maps, each map shows its start point. In addition numbered directions have been placed on each map. The numbers correspond to the directions within the walks.

Walk 1 – Lille Centre and South

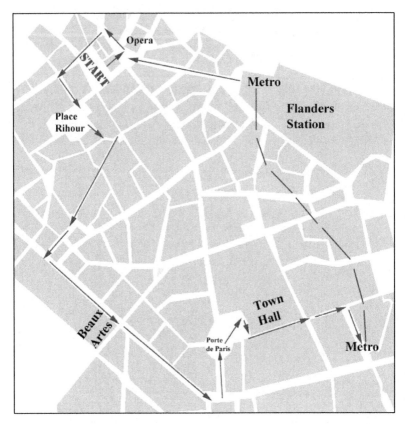

Route Overview

Start this walk in the Grand Place, which is officially called the Place du Général de Gaulle.

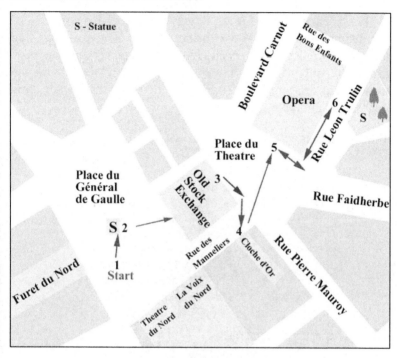

Map 1

Grand Place

Charles De Gaulle was born in Lille and is very much a local hero. He was a minister in the French Parliament when World War II erupted. He campaigned against the infamous armistice agreed by France in 1940, which effectively abandoned Northern France to Germany and put a puppet government called the Vichy Government in place over the rest of France.

De Gaulle escaped to London where he led the Free French Forces in World War II, and he used the BBC to stir his compatriots to resist the Nazis. The Free French Forces fought against Germany overseas and helped the French Resistance.

After the war, De Gaulle became the president of France for a decade in the sixties.

The Grand Place is a lovely square surrounded by handsome buildings. It was originally the wheat market and later became the commercial centre of town. Today it is very much the hub of life in Lille. In spring it hosts a colourful flower market, and at Christmas it is turned into a fairyland with lights and decorations.

The Goddess

Map 1.1 - Walk over to the fountain and statue in the middle of the square.

This statue at the top of this tall column is known as Déesse which means The Goddess in English. She is celebrating Lille's victory against the Austrians in 1792 when they put Lille under siege.

The French started a war with Austria during the French Revolutionary Wars, a period when France seemed to be at war with most of Europe. The Austrians responded in kind and marched into France and arrived at the gates of Lille. The Austrian commander issued a summons, stating that he would spare Lille if the city surrendered.

The Mayor of Lille responded with:

> *Lille and its inhabitants*
> *have renewed their oath of loyalty to the nation,*
> *to live free or to die,*
> *and that they will not surrender*

The city stood firm and held the Austrians at bay.

During the nine day siege the Austrians bombarded the city with twenty-four cannons. The Lille artillery responded – from the ramparts they fired back and rushed to bolster the most vulnerable parts of the city's defences. It's said that women and children of Lille raced to where the cannon-fire was landing to extinguish the fires as quickly as possible, while the menfolk defended the walls.

The Austrians fell as the Lille cannons roared back again and again, but the Lillois also died in huge numbers. Civilians burned to death despite the bravest of efforts to hold back the fires. A quarter of Lille burned to the ground. However the Austrians finally fell back and left.

Given how often Lille was overpowered and annexed by the various surrounding countries over the centuries, it's not surprising they put up a statue to their victory. However it did take them over fifty years to get around to it – Déesse was installed in 1845.

Déesse is holding a firebrand in one hand, ready to light the cannons used to repel the Austrians. Her crown represents the ramparts of the city wall. She is pointing to an inscription on the column beneath her, where you can see the Mayor's famous response to the Austrian demand for surrender. She was sculpted by Dutchman Théophile Bra who is quoted as saying:

> *"Lille! Lille ! Lille! She is a woman whose forehead must bear the imprint of the calm and obstinate courage of the Flemings.*
>
> *I will make her left hand speak, which will imperiously point to our heroic reply at her feet. This is not all: the first shot that will leave the trench; it will require a more eloquent response. Ah ! Ah! La voici ! There she is! This other hand armed with a blaster will be ready to answer the Austrian insolence. Yes, yes, that's it, I see my statue of Lille, I see it."*

It's said that he modelled Déesse's face on Marie-Josephe, the wife of Monsieur Bigo-Danel who was the Mayor at the time and who commissioned the statue.

During World War I, Déesse had to witness the German Changing of the Guard every day at noon Berlin Time. The German soldiers marched down Rue Nationale to drums and pipes, and the ceremony took place at the foot of the Goddess – probably all done to intimidate and humiliate the local population.

Stand face to face with Déesse and turn right. You will see the La Voix du Nord building.

La Voix du Nord

The very Flemish style building with the stepped gable is now the headquarters of La Voix du Nord, the leading local newspaper. It started life as an underground paper of the French Resistance in 1941 when the first 65 issues were secretly published. It is now the largest newspaper in Northern France.

If you count the number of windows on the front of the building you will find there are 28, one for each of the local editions of the daily newspaper. There is a region name etched under each of the windows. On top of the building, you can see the three lovely golden statues of Artois, Flanders, and Halnault, which were the three local provinces of Northern France long ago.

Below the ladies is a balcony surrounded by traditional workers of Norther France, fishermen, sailors, farmers and miners. The words below the balcony proclaim:

Défendre le travail dans la région du Nord

Defend the work of the North

Now take a look at the building on the right-hand side of the Voix du Nord with the double staircase.

Le Grand'Garde

This is now the Theatre du Nord. It was built way back in the 1700's by order of the French king, Louis XIV, who had just annexed Lille. Louis was not completely convinced of the loyalty of his new French subjects, so he decided to bring one of his garrisons into the centre of town for security. They were called the Royal Guard, and housed in this building.

Louis XIV was of course known as the Sun King, and if you look up at the triangular pediment of this building you can see the sun flanked by the coats of arms of France and Lille. Even the weathervane symbolizes the sun.

If the stairways are open to the public, pop up for a good view of the Grand Place.

Return to stand face to face with Déesse again, and this time turn round to find the Furet du Nord.

Furet du Nord

It's a bookshop which was at one time the largest in the world. It originally opened in what had been an old fur shop in nearby Rue de la Vieille-Comédie. The bookshop owner decided to keep the original shop's name, Furet du Nord, The Northern Ferret. The furrier had worked with rabbit skins, and the rabbits were traditionally hunted with ferrets.

Face Déesse again, and behind her and slightly to the right you will see the ornate Vieille Bourse.

The Old Stock Exchange (Vielle Bourse)

The Old Stock Exchange is appropriately housed in one of the oldest buildings in Lille and it's one of the most beautiful. It was originally built to give the traders some shelter from the weather of Northern France. Prior to its construction they had to make deals outside - even in the rain. The merchants petitioned the Count of Flanders and permission was granted to build the Exchange.

It's our good fortune that they decided that since they were building a Stock Exchange, they should make it a good one. It's actually twenty-four identical houses built to surround a central courtyard. At the top of the bell tower you can see a golden Mercury – he was the God of Trade.

Above the door you can see Lille's coat of arms which has two lions guarding a fleur-de-lis. Right round the exterior of the building you can see sculptures of various cultures, like the Turkish turbaned heads representing the exotic eastern markets.

There are four entrances into the courtyard, one on each side of the building.

Map 1.2 - Go through the archway to reach the courtyard

Once in the courtyard try to imagine it as it once was. The ground level was busy with very upmarket shops, and the traders would make their deals in the courtyard or perhaps under the arcade.

The Stock Exchange has been beautifully restored. Sponsors were needed and many large French businesses helped with hard cash – and they are commemorated on the courtyard walls.

Have a look round the arcade itself and you will see memorials to the scientists of the time who were revolutionizing European life – including Pasteur. He became the Dean of Lille University, and it was in the Institut Pasteur de Lille that the BCG vaccine against tuberculosis was developed.

Each of the four entrances to the courtyard is decorated with two cherubs who hold a commemoration of the history or business of the Stock Exchange:

```
Grateful Industry 1853
Courts and Chamber of Commerce
Inventive Genius
Honour at Work
```

The year 1853 was the year that Napoleon III approved the request from Lille that a statue of his uncle, Emperor Napoleon, should be erected in the courtyard. The large statue which was erected depicted Napoleon Bonaparte in full emperor costume. It was removed at the end of the twentieth century and moved to the Palais des Beaux-Arts, and it's a shame they did not replace it with a copy. You might decide to visit the art museum later in this walk; if you do you will get a chance to see the original.

Nowadays you will find second-hand booksellers stalls in place. They are fun to rummage around and you might find a bargain. There are often chess matches going on and apparently even dancing demonstrations in summer, so who knows what you will find.

Map 1.3 - Leave the courtyard by the archway which lies directly opposite the archway you entered by. It will take you into another large square called the Place du Theatre.

Turn right as you enter the square to reach the end of the Vielle Bourse. Turn right into Rue des Manneliers but take only a few steps.

A la Cloche d'Or

On the left-hand side of this street is a small jeweller's shop. Look up to the first floor to see the lovely Art Nouveau shop-front bearing the name "A la Cloche d'Or", which means "At the Golden Bell". Oddly the Bell is the one part of the façade decoration which is not golden.

There are not too many Art Nouveau buildings in Lille, so this little example is much loved by the locals.

Map 1.4 - Backtrack to Place du Theatre and opposite you stands the very grand Opera House.

L'Opera

This is the second incarnation of the Opera House. The original burned down in 1903, but was replaced by an even more sumptuous building in a very French style.

It took more than a decade to build and rather embarrassingly it was officially opened by the Germans in 1914 after Lille had been invaded. The Germans named it the "Deutsches Theater" and it was opened in a grand ceremony in the presence of the Crown Prince Rupert of Bavaria.

When the Germans finally left in 1918, the German artists who had run the theatre made sure they destroyed all the sets and equipment as a parting gift. After World War I the Opera was re-opened by the French.

Look up to find Apollo and his muses. Apollo is of course the God of Music. On the left of the façade music is represented by musicians, and on the right drama is represented by a sculpture of Tragedy. Even the doors themselves are decorated with dramatic golden faces over musical instruments.

Unless you buy a ticket for a performance, or are lucky to be in Lille on one of the rare open days, you will have to imagine its monumental staircase, and its wonderful interior gilded in bronze, gold, marble and dazzling crystals.

We are actually very lucky that both the Vielle Bourse and the Opera House are still standing. At the start of WWI, German bombardments fell as close as Rue Faidherbe which lies just to the east of both buildings

Map 1.5 - When you are ready to move on, face the Opera and go down the right hand side and you will see the life-size statue of Leon Trulin on the other side of the road.

Léon Trulin

Léon Trulin was a Belgian who came to Lille and started work in a factory to help the family finances – he had seven

siblings.   He was just 18 when WWI began and Lille was occupied.   He escaped to Britain and tried to join the Belgian army in exile, but he was turned down because of his height.

Not to be stopped, he returned to Lille and setup an organization of teenagers who spied on the Germans.   Leon sent the reports back to Great Britain.   The organisation was called "Noel Lurtin", an anagram of his name.

He and two of his colleagues were caught and sentenced to death.   His two friends were allowed to live but Trulin was shot in a ditch in front of the Citadel – Lille's great fortress.

There are several statues to Trulin around Lille.   This one has an inscription of his last written words:

> *I forgive everyone, friend and foe.*
> *I show them mercy*
> *because of the mercy they have not shown me'*

Map 1.6 - Return to the front of the Opera House.

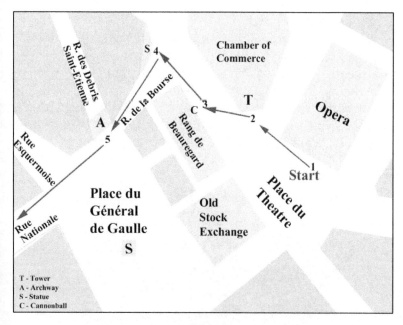

Map 2

Map 2.1 - Face the Opera and turn left to reach the Chamber of Commerce.

Chamber of Commerce

This was the new Stock Exchange, built about the same time as the first Opera House burned down. Its high bell-tower represents the power of the merchant cities of Northern Europe. It has a clock on each side of the tower, and the 25 bells chime out every quarter hour.

On the hour they play the "P'tit Quinquin", a much loved lullaby written in Lille, which tells the story of a poor lace-maker from Lille who is trying to get her baby Narcisse to sleep. So if you are around at that time, have a listen.

Map 2.2 - Opposite the Chamber of Commerce is the Rang de Beauregard. Cross the square to reach it.

Rang de Beauregard

When this terrace of identical houses was being designed, Lille had strict rules on building design as they wanted to keep the centre of town beautiful. New buildings had to complement the design of their neighbours and only brick and stone could be used in construction. So to be in line with the neighbouring Old Stock Exchange, this terrace is just three storeys high, and the outside walls are beautifully embellished.

The Bellringer

Find number 13 on the left hand corner of the building and you will also find a sweet little statue beneath a large bell. The statue is from the eighteenth century and his job was to ring the bell when the Stock Exchange opened or closed.

Face the Bellringer and turn right towards the other end of the Rang de Beauregard. As you near the end you will find Morel & Fils

Morel & Fils

This shop started life as a lingerie shop, but as the market for lingerie dropped the family first converted it into a bookshop and finally into a café. However they kept some of the original decoration and mannequins from the lingerie shop in place, so it's an interesting place to stop for refreshment.

Have a good look at the brickwork, and you will see small cannon balls blasted into Lille during the Austrian siege. One of them has been decorated by Monsieur Morel with a wine cork and painted pink to make it look like a breast. It's on the second floor, above the "S" of "Fils". There are two other undecorated cannonballs high above the "E" of "Morel".

Map 2.3 - Walk to the end of the Rang de Beauregard.

You will see an ornate building with pink stonework on the other side of Rue de la Bourse. Many of the old buildings in Lille have little angels adorning the windows. If you look closely you will see that some of them are hugging each other and others are giving the cold shoulder. The ones hugging each others are on windows belonging to the same residence.

Map 2.4 - Face the angels and turn left to go down Rue de la Bourse.

As you enter the Grand Place again, you will see a very large archway on your right. Behind the archway is Rue des Debris Saint-Etienne.

Rue des Debris Saint-Etienne

Saint Etienne was a church which was destroyed by cannonballs fired by the Austrian army during the siege. The rubble lay in this area for ten years but finally it was cleared and Rue des Debris Saint-Etienne was built where it stood.

Where possible the rubble was recycled into the new buildings which were built on the grounds of the church and cemetery. The two sandstone columns you see on either side of the archway were saved from the rubble and were incorporated into the street entrance.

Map 2.5 - Walk past the archway, and keeping Déesse on your left walk straight ahead into Rue Nationale.

Walk down to the crossroads with Rue de Pas and Rue Jean Roisin.

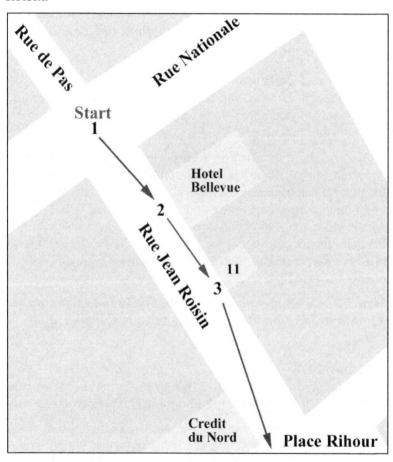

Map 3

Map 3.1 - Take the next left into Rue Jean Roisin.

Rue Jean Roisin

As you know from the Potted History, Lille once had many canals which were used to control the water from the marshy river Deûle, and to transport goods across Lille.

One of the canals was called the Poissonceaux Canal and it ran along this street. It was filled in and this street was laid over its route.

As you enter the street you will find the Grand Hotel Bellevue on your left.

Grand Hotel Bellevue

Its claim to fame is that this is where the musical prodigy Mozart stayed when he was taken on tour by his father at the tender age of just nine.

He was paraded around Europe for three years, both to show off his talent and to make some cash by performing in front of dukes and barons, emperors and empresses, and kings and queens. He was even tested when he visited London - he was given a sheet of complex music and to the amazement of his audience, was able to play it immediately on the keyboard. Mozart stayed in this hotel for four weeks when he fell ill during the gruelling schedule.

Map 3.2 – Continue along Rue Jean Roisin to reach number 11 on your left-hand side – it's the third building along from the hotel.

Number 11

Look down to spot an inscription of "Anno 1771" on the brickwork – that is the year the building was constructed.

Those pavement-level windows and that inscription were part of the building's original ground floor which stood alongside the Poissonceaux canal. When the Rue Jean Roison was laid over the canal, the street-level was raised and the original ground floor of this building was mostly buried.

Map 3.3 – Continue to the end of the street where you will find the Credit du Nord Bank on your right.

Credit du Nord Bank

During World War I when Lille was occupied by the Germans, many of the buildings in the town centre were requisitioned by the German Administration.

The old Credit du Nord building which stood here became the office of the German Commander, General von Heinrich. It was there that he met with the Mayor and Bishop of Lille every day to deal with running the city.

The Credit du Nord Bank building which stands here now was built after World War II.

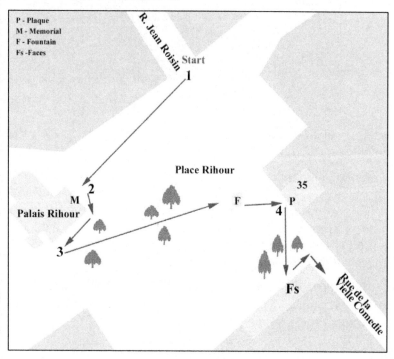

Map 4

Map 4.1 - Just beyond the bank is Place Rihour. This square is where the Christmas market is to be found.

As you enter this busy square you will see the large war memorial on your right. Make your way towards it.

The War Memorial

It is called Melancolia and it commemorates the fate of the people who suffered dreadfully in World War I.

Once Belgium had been gobbled up, Lille was just a stone's throw away. The German army marched in on October 13th 1914 and occupied the town for four years. The battlefront was so close to Lille that for three years they lived with the sound of cannon-fire every day, and huge numbers of soldiers marched through on a regular basis.

The German occupying forces in WWI were brutal; they took anything of value, especially food and blankets. Rape was common and minor misdemeanours often resulted in execution.

The poignant carvings on the memorial show the townspeople being taken prisoner by the Germans. At the worst point, two thousand people were taken from their homes daily and deported to Germany as slave labour. The prisoners and townspeople showed their spirit by singing the Marseillaise as the trains left Lille heading eastwards.

The Germans finally left Lille on October 17th 1918 and the British army was welcomed with tears and joy. The British General was made an honorary citizen of Lille.

The mayor made a speech which summed up those terrible times,

> *For four years we have been like miners buried alive,*
> *listening for the sound of the rescuers' picks,*
> *then all at once the dark gallery opens*
> *and we see the light"*

Map 4.2 - Behind the memorial is what is left of the Palais Rihour.

Palais Rihour

The building with the octagonal tower is all that is left of the Palais Rihour, built in 1453 for the Duke of Burgundy who ruled Flanders at the time. It was originally very much larger, a huge square building with a central courtyard.

Its most famous moment was "The Feast of the Pheasant" which was the incredibly lavish climax to an eighteen day jamboree in the middle ages. The feast was hosted by the Duke of Burgundy on behalf of the Pope, to persuade the lords and knights to saddle up and rescue Constantinople from the Turks. One of the many over-the-top amusements laid on for the guests was an enormous pie which had twenty-four musicians inside. The guests enjoyed the party, but declined to go to war.

Famous visitors to the palace include Henry VIII of England and Louis XV of France. Henry VIII demonstrated his skill in music when he visited, playing various instruments including the lute and the harp.

The building later became Lille's town hall, but was badly damaged over the centuries and was finally wrecked by a fire in 1916 during the German occupation. However, what survived has been restored and now holds the tourist office on the ground floor. It sits in the former Guard room which has a vaulted ceiling.

You can visit the Salle du Conclave which is worth seeing. You need to climb the stairway - the gate lies just beside the entrance to the Tourist Office. If it's closed just ask at the office when it will be open – they shut for lunch.

When you climb up you will reach a second vaulted hall which is the Salle du Conclave. Find the little room off to the left which was the sacristy. Go in to see the colourful stained glass windows.

Map 4.3 - Once back outside, approach the small pyramid fountain in the middle of the square.

Make your way to number 35 which lies behind the fountain and near the Metro entrance.

Voltaire Plaque

You will find a plaque on the wall there, commemorating Voltaire's play Mahomet. It was put there by the Friends of Lille.

It was a very controversial play in which Voltaire poked fun at the prophet Mohammed. Voltaire was a very outspoken writer despite the risk he ran of arrest, as writing was heavily censored in France at that time. He often wrote against intolerance and religion, and this play has been interpreted as an indirect attack on the Catholic Church.

It's been suggested that he decided to debut the play in Lille, because if things got too hot, he could vanish into Flanders. In fact his play was a success in Lille but was banned by parliament a year later after it was performed in Paris.

Map 4.4 - Face away from Voltaire's plaque.

Cross diagonally left to find a colourful building lined with faces sticking their tongues out.

Walk around the left-hand side of the building into Rue de la Vieille Comédie.

Rue de la Vieille Comédie

The street gets its name, Street of the Old Comedy, from the old theatre which stood here but which is sadly long gone. It was where Voltaire's play "Mahomet" was first performed back in 1741.

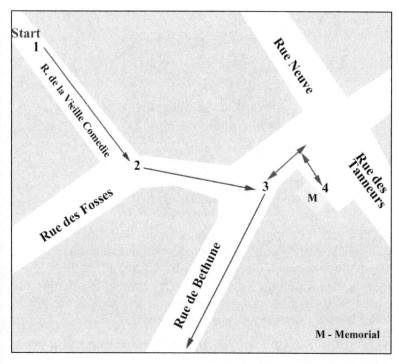

Map 5

Map 5.1 - Walk along Rue de la Vieille Comédie. Ignore the Rue des Fosses on your right.

Map 5.2 - Continue to the next junction with Rue de Bethune.

Map 5.3 - You will shortly be turning into Rue de Bethune. Before you do that, take a few steps left, and then turn right to find the Parvis des Justes on the wall.

Parvis des Justes

You are standing at the "Forecourt of the Righteous", and you will see the plaque and fresco put there to commemorate those citizens of Lille recognised by Israel as the "Righteous among the Nations". This is the highest civilian distinction awarded to non-Jewish people who, at the risk of their own lives, helped Jews persecuted by the Nazis.

Map 5.4 - Now backtrack around the corner and walk straight ahead into Rue de Béthune.

It was bombed heavily during WWII and was later rebuilt as a long pedestrianized street – it is the main shopping street in Lille. If you feel in need of some shopping therapy you can find something here, however be warned that it gets very busy at the weekend!

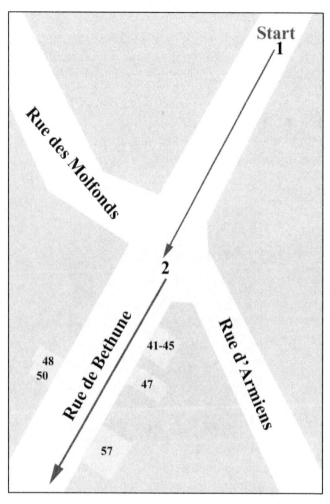

Map 6

Map 6.1 – The first part of this street is a bit boring, so walk briskly along Rue de Bethune to reach a crossroads with Rue des Molfonds and Rue d'Armiens.

Map 6.2 - Walk straight ahead staying on Rue de Bethune.

Rue de Bethune

If shopping doesn't really interest you, you can still take a minute or two to look above the shops as you stroll along. You will find a nice collection of Art Deco/Nouveau embellishments as you do.

Number 41-45

Number 41-45 on your left has a lovely door and bow windows framed by twirling foliage.

Number 47

Just two buildings further along at number 47 is a set of bow windows with unusual protruding brickwork.

Number 48

A little further along on the other side of the street is number 48 with a façade full of ornate iron balconies. Just next door to that are more iron balconies accompanied by vines and foliage around the windows.

Number 57

Not too far along you will find number 57 on your left, with more iron balconies and bold stonework.

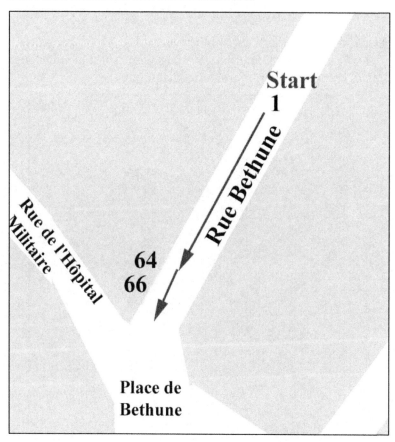

Map 7

Map 7.1 Continue towards the end of Rue de Bethune to reach number 64 on your right.

Number 64

Here you will find Maison Gilbert – it has a splendid rounded pediment right at the top which shouts out the building's name.

Number 66

Just next door is another building with iron balconies and lots of stonework with floral embellishments.

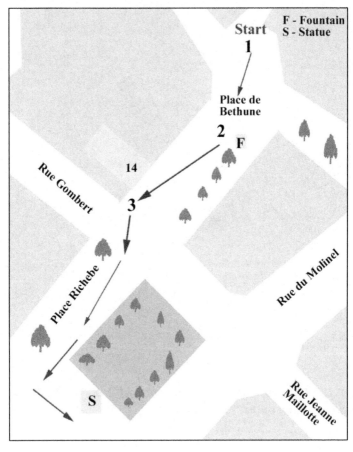

Map 8

Map 8.1 - You will reach a crossroads. Beyond that lies the Place de Bethune, a long tree-lined square.

As you enter the square you will find a pretty little fountain on the left-hand side.

Wallace Fountain

Lille has only one Wallace fountain but Paris has many more. They were donated by Richard Wallace who was an avid art collector from London but who lived and died in Paris. His vast art collection is on show at the Wallace Collection in London.

Wallace decided to give Paris a set of fountains so that fresh clean water would be available to everyone. Being artistic he wanted his fountains to be beautiful, and he decided to decorate them with four ladies, Kindness, Charity, Simplicity and Sobriety. Each lady stands in a slightly different position. A chained goblet was even provided for the drinker. Wallace donated fifty to Paris and others were sprinkled around France, including Lille.

Map 8.2 – Continue Walking through the square.

Further along on your right hand side and near the next crossroads you can see another example of this area's love of decoration – this time of a face and two horns of plenty at number 14.

Map 8.3 – Make your way over the next crossroads. On the other side of it stands Place Richebé which has a little park on the left.

Walk to the end of the park and turn left to find the equestrian statue of General Faidherbe.

General Faidherbe

He was born in Lille and had a long military career. He was the governor of Senegal in Africa, but was recalled to France to be commander-in-chief of the Army of the North after

Napoleon III was defeated by the Prussians in the Franco-Prussian war.

That was a war which the French started fully expecting to win, but they quickly found they had bitten off more than they could chew. The Prussians won and France lost the Alsace as a consequence. However Faidherbe and the Army of the North held their ground better than most of the French army, so the General is seen as a hero. The ladies at the bottom of the statue represent Lille extolling the virtues of the General during the battle of Bapaume in 1871 against the Prussians which the French won.

Times have changed though, and many people now object to the fact that one of Lille's main streets is named after General Faidherbe, due to his period as governor of Senegal. There is even talk of renaming Rue Faidherbe, which runs from Flanders Station to the Grand Place, to something less controversial.

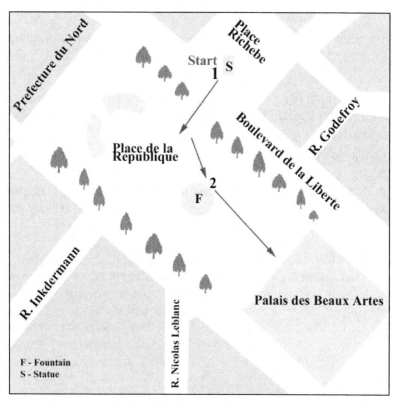

Map 9

Map 9.1 - Cross the road in front of the General, Boulevard de la Liberté, to enter the Place de la République.

Place de la République

This large square was originally called Place Napoleon III and is built on the old town fortifications. It has a much more French appearance and feel to it than the older Flemish squares you have just visited.

In the centre is a large fountain with a modern piece of art in the middle, "Groupe des trois". It's not really clear what the three pieces are, but that's modern art.

To your right is the amphitheatre – which is both an entrance to the Metro and a venue for street theatre. Beyond that is the Prefecture du Nord, which is situated in Lille because Lille is the Capital of Northern France.

Map 9.2 - To your left is the Palais des Beaux Artes which is well worth a visit. If you want to visit, make your way to the entrance.

However if you don't want to visit the museum, return to Boulevard de la Liberté. Turn right and walk along the Boulevard to the nearest corner of the Palais des Beaux Artes. Continue this walk from "Boulevard de la Liberté" on page 57.

Palais des Beaux Artes

This building was founded by Napoleon I. The museum's collection was originally displayed inside a church, then as it got bigger it was moved to the town hall, and finally to this lovely building which was built in the late nineteenth century. Lille was one of the lucky 15 French cities to become custodians of the works of art lifted from churches and conquests of Napoleon I's army.

It has been renovated and is a pleasant place to wander around, with lots of space, columns, and grand staircases. It has works by many of the big names, Raphael, Donatello, Van Dyck, Rembrandt, Goya, El Greco, Toulouse Lautrec, Delacroix, Rubens and Rodin.

The museum is the largest French museum outside of Paris, beaten only by the Louvre. It is home to a lot of paintings which are worth seeing; however it's a very big museum. So if you plan a single visit, focus on the highlights – the museum will provide you with a good map of the collection and a list of suggested targets. You can also of course make use of the offered Visioguide as long as you have your passport with you for identification.

The paintings are on the first floor, and the ground floor holds statues and temporary exhibitions. Here are some personal favourites, but the Visioguide will take your round many more.

Great Shadow – Rodin

This striking muscular figure actually has two brothers in other museums. They are stand-alone versions of the Three Shadow figures Rodin placed on his "Gates of Hell", a huge work which was inspired by Dante's description of the entrance to the Inferno.

Through me the way into the suffering city,
Through me the way to the eternal pain,
Through me the way that runs among the lost.
Justice urged on my high artificer;
My Maker was Divine authority,
The highest Wisdom, and the primal Love.
Before me nothing but eternal things
Were made, and I endure eternally
Abandon every hope, who enter here.

Rodin is quoted as saying:

"For a whole year I lived with Dante,
with him alone,
drawing the eight circles of his inferno."

His Three Shadow figures stand at the top of the "Gates of Hell" and point down to those dreadful words:

"Abandon all hope, who enter here"

Cleopatra - Gauthier

This is a very sensual statue and depicts Cleopatra ending her life. It was originally thought to be the work of Darcq who came from Lille, however when the statue was cleaned Charles Gauthier's signature appeared.

Les Vieilles – Goya

This is one of the most memorable paintings in the collection. It shows two ancient but well-dressed ladies looking into a mirror, and perhaps not seeing the ravages of time. The book being looked at says "Que Tal", or "How are you". Behind them stands Time, waiting with a broom to sweep them away. Perhaps Goya was pointing out the pointlessness of the eternal search for beauty.

Descent from the Cross – Rubens

This is a favourite theme of Rubens. It shows the sadness and heartbreak of those waiting for Christ's end, including of course Mary Magdalene who is depicted with blond hair.

The Ecstasy of Mary Magdalene – Rubens

This painting is based on the legend of her life after the crucifixion, when she lived in a cave in the desert and devoted herself to God.

Houses of Parliament – Monet

Monet stayed in London and actually painted this scene of The Palace of Westminster about a dozen times. The paintings are sprinkled across Europe.

Le Dénombrement de Bethléem – Breughel

Like most of Breughel's paintings, this one tells us many stories. It's set in a Flemish village in winter, and you can see the country folk working and carousing, the children playing, and even a pig being slaughtered.

Breughel transposed the Nativity story from Bethlehem to Flanders. You can see a hut outside the sumptuous Inn, and figures representing Joseph and Mary in search for shelter from the cold. Mary is in blue, the traditional colour of the Virgin.

Cows – Van Gogh

This painting by Van Gogh makes me smile. It looks like it should be in a children's book about farming. However Van Gogh completed this painting just before he committed suicide, so perhaps it wasn't his most happy work.

The Fall of the Damned – Bouts

This is a frightening painting by Dutch painter Dieric Bouts. It shows the horror and pain of those heading to hell on the Day of Judgment. He also painted "The Way to Paradise" which hangs next to it. It's a contrast but it isn't nearly as memorable.

Medea - Delacroix

This painting shows Medea about to kill her two sons as an act of revenge against Jason their father, who had abandoned her for another woman. It caused a sensation when it was exhibited, as the imminent murder of the innocent children shocked people.

The Temptation of Saint Anthony – Teniers

Saint Anthony headed to the Egyptian desert to pray and devote himself to God. Many artists have painted his legendary Temptation by the Devil, when he is offered food, wine, and sex to pull him away from God. This painting makes me smile as it looks like he is being offered a Martini.

The Wolf of Gubbio – Merson

This is the story of a wolf which terrorised the city of Gubbio by killing the livestock and the people, until it was tamed by St Francis of Assisi. The painting shows the wolf visiting the townspeople of Gubbio for food, as promised by St Francis if the wolf stopped its slaughter. It does look a bit more like a friendly dog than a ferocious wolf.

Vestal Virgins Old and New Jean Raoux

The first painting shows us the Vestal Virgins of Rome clustered around and tending the sacred fire which must never be allowed to go out. If it did disaster would fall on Rome.

The second painting is of virgins in Raoux's time, who are not clustered around anything, but are intent on learning and studying the arts.

Regardless of the message or moral of the paintings, both are very pretty.

When you have had enough art, you could pop down to the bar/restaurant in the basement to recharge your batteries.

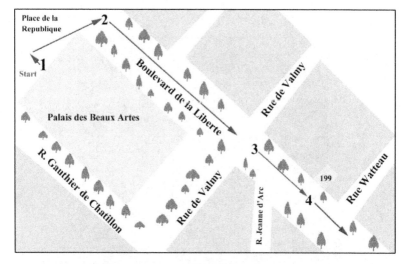

Map 10

Map 10.1 - Exit the museum into the Place de la Republique.

With the museum behind you, go round the museum to your right, into Boulevard de la Liberté.

Boulevard de la Liberté

The Boulevard is lined with plane trees and it follows the line of the old city wall. The road is lined with many stylish houses.

Map 10.2 – Continue along the Boulevard and cross the junction with Rue de Valmy.

Map 10.3 - Walk along the Boulevard to number 199 on your left.

Boulevard de la Liberté 199

If you like art-deco/nouveau architecture, take a look at number 199 on your left, which has a red brick facade with a red central window and balcony.

The architect was Horace Pouillet who was inspired by both Art Nouveau and Art Deco styles. His name is on this pretty house; you can find it below and to the right of the large central window.

Boulevard de la Liberté 201

Just next door at number 201 is another interesting Art Deco building, this time by Ernest Willoqueaux. The dark moulded doors are particularly eye-catching.

The architect's name is etched on the stonework on the first floor between the balconies.

Map 10.4 - Continue down Boulevard de la Liberté passing Rue Watteau on your left.

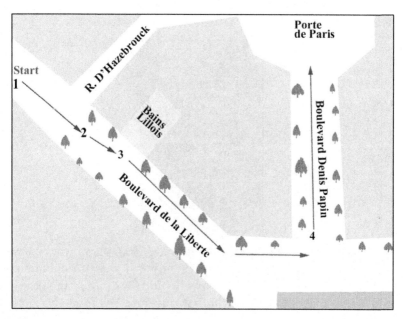

Map 11

Map 11.1 – Walk along the boulevard and pass Rue d'Hazebrouck on the left.

Map 11.2 – A little further along you will reach number 219 - the old Bains Lillois.

Bains Lillois

This was an old public swimming pool from the early twentieth century. Internally it's now a modern apartment block, but they have kept the lovely old 1903 facade including the Bains Lillois lettering, the balcony, and the four entrance columns.

The building just next door on the left is also very pretty with its blue-green stone work and iron balcony.

Map 11.3 - Continue in the same direction. The boulevard will swing to the left, and you should then turn left into Boulevard Denis Papin.

Boulevard Denis Papin

This is said to be the shortest boulevard in the world, just 110 metres in length.

If you are in need of refreshments you might want to have a look at number 9 on the right hand side, where you will find L'impertinente, a much loved teashop.

Map 11.4 – The Boulevard will take you towards the Porte de Paris. As you near the Porte you can see the Town Hall tower behind it diagonally right.

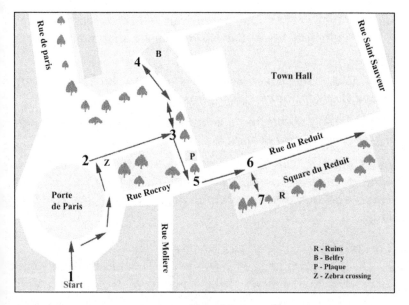

Map 12

Porte de Paris

As you know, Lille was heavily fortified with a defensive wall which surrounded the city. The walls were guarded by a number of gates. It's a shame but most of the town walls were demolished in the name of progress, and only a few of the gates have survived. This is one of them. When the walls were demolished this eye-catching gate was preserved, and it is now in the middle of a traffic roundabout.

This is a very ornate gate because it is really a triumphal arch which was built to celebrate Louis XIV's capture of Lille. He entered the city through the previous gate which stood here, the Porte des Malades, so named because it was used to reach the hospital. It was replaced by this gate after Louis's victory.

Right at the top of the gate you see Victory preparing to crown Louis with a laurel wreath. On one side is Hercules and

61

on the other is Mars, the god of war. All this decoration was added just in case anyone didn't realize that Louis was in charge.

Map 12.1 - When you want to move on, make your way round the right-hand side of the gate.

Map 12.2 - You will find a zebra crossing which you should use to cross the main road.

Head towards the Town Hall, which is the large building behind the trees and to the right of the high tower. The Town Hall has a little roundabout in front of it circled by flags.

Town Hall

The new town hall replaced the old Town Hall which stood in Place Rihour and which Lille outgrew. It was built after WWI - and Lille decided to use its construction as a means of improving and regenerating this part of town which was very deprived and run down. The architect produced a very functional building but also incorporated the lovely Flemish style of gabled roofs and stonework to make it an attractive building as well.

Inside there is a long, long gallery which runs the length of the building, and which is decorated with impressive marble and ironwork columns. The idea is that the long gallery should be seen as a "street", and visitors would walk down the street to visit the adjoining side galleries.

You can visit during the week, but it's closed at the weekend. If you get inside, go upstairs to visit the Erro Room, it contains a very colourful mural by Icelandic artist Erro and it tells the story of Lyderic and Phinaert, the founders of Lille.

The wicked giant Phinaert murdered the Prince of Dijon and most of his party when they tried to cross his land. The Prince's wife escaped to the forest and had a vision of the

Virgin Mary who told her that her son would wreak revenge. Sure enough The Prince's wife had a son and managed to hide him in the forest before Phinaert caught her.

The baby was raised by a hermit and was named Lyderic. When he was 18 he returned to challenge Phinaert, and killed him and all his family. The locals were so impressed by the strength and might of Lyderic that a community gathered round his court and Lille was born.

Also look into the office of Roger Salengro if you can. He was a soldier and POW during World War I. After the war he became a socialist politician and became mayor of Lille in 1925. He suffered a vicious attack by the right wing press who claimed he was a deserter rather than a POW. He was finally driven to suicide in 1939. This caused the French Government to put a law in place to outlaw such libel. His office has been left untouched as a memorial and is full of period furniture.

Map 12.3 - When you leave the Town Hall, turn right to reach the Belfry.

The Belfry

Stone effigies of Lyderic and Phnaert support the belfry, or the "skyscraper of Flanders" as it is sometimes known, as it is 104 meters high. The tower is supported by 270 cement piles and actually weighs more than the Eiffel Tower.

You can go up - the entrance is an unmarked wooden door just beside Lyderic and Phinaert. It doesn't really advertise itself but just push it open to get in. Climb the steps for the first part and you then have a choice of using the elevator or continuing to climb – I would advise the lift as it is a very, very high tower. You can also hire binoculars and an audio guide to get the most out of your visit but they are not really necessary.

They only allow about eighteen viewers up the tower at once, so depending on the time of day you might have to wait a bit before being allowed up. However there are some posters and information boards to browse whilst waiting your turn.

On a clear day you can see for thirty kilometres and at night a light beams out across the city and the countryside. From the top you get a very good bird's-eye view of the Porte de Paris. You can see the pretty knot garden around the gate which is not really visible from ground level. Also spot the little metro trains which run not far from the tower – you will be on one soon.

The tower is built on the site of the La Liberté bar, which is where Pierre Degeyter composed L'Internationale, a very well known "socialist" anthem. You probably know the tune once you hear it. There is a good rendition on YouTube at

https://www.youtube.com/watch?v=EpgrO-tieGM

In 1950, Tele Lille moved in to the tower to transmit to the whole region, and was France's first regional television station. The station was in residence for seven years.

When you have had enough of the view you can take the lift down, but it's an easy descent by the stairs.

Map 12.4 - Exit the tower and turn left to walk past the Town Hall.

As you reach its end you will see a memorial to Mayor Salengro on your left.

Map 12.5 - When you reach Rue de Reduit, turn left to walk along the side of the Town Hall.

Map 12.6 - Not too far along you will see the green Square du Reduit on the other side of the road. Cross over to enter the little park.

Square du Reduit

Against the far wall of the little park you will find all that remains of the Tournai Gate which once stood near here. It was demolished along with many other parts of the old fortifications at the start of the twentieth century.

Map 12.7 - Exit the Park and turn right to continue along Rue de Reduit to reach the end of the park.

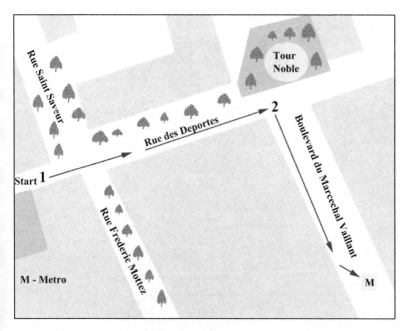

Map 13

Map 13.1 - Continue down Rue de Reduit and cross the junction into Rue de Deportees.

Go past the first rather ugly building on your left and you will find the Tour Noble.

Tour Noble

This tower went up as part of the towns fortifications during the 100 year war, which was a series of battles and wars which lasted just short of a century between England and France.

At stake was the throne of France. Both sides felt they had a claim, remember that the English throne had been taken over by the French in 1066. The English ruling family, the Plantagenets, still had family connections to the French royal family. So when there was no clear line of inheritance, like any other family they squabbled, except in this case it involved two armies. The English actually had the better claim except it was through a woman. France invoked the Salic law, which doesn't allow inheritance through the female line. Being female, my vote is for England.

Anyway during this long running battle, the Burgundians built 65 towers around Lille to keep the French out – yes Burgundy was on England's side.

This tower has walls three feet thick and is half underground. However Lille was not very good at holding back the enemy and the city was soon in French hands. The tower became an ammunitions depot.

It became a memorial to the resistance of World War II and was opened by Général de Gaulle in 1959. Inside is a stone urn which contains ashes from the Nazi death camps. Outside, you can see a sculpture to commemorate the victims on the tower wall.

Map 13.2 - Opposite the tower is Boulevard du Maréchal Vaillant. Go down this street to find the Lille Grand Palais Metro station. Its entrance sits on an island at the far end of the street.

The Lille metro was the first in the world to be completely automated. If you don't have a city card, buy a ticket at the machines.

The Metro

The French use the final station names of a metro line to identify where the line goes to. The two end stations of this metro line are Saint-Philibert and CH Dron. You want to go in direction CH Dron to return to town. The lines are well signposted, so make sure you are on the right track to go in the right direction. Take the next train to go two stations north and get off at Gare Lille Flandres. This will save you a rather boring walk.

The metro station has several exits, so when you leave the train follow the signs to Gare Lille Flandres and you will exit at the front of the old train station.

When you reach the front of Flanders station, stop to take a quick look at it.

Gare de Lille Flandres

What you are looking at is actually the old Gare du Nord station from Paris. They dismantled it in 1867 and then re-erected it here. It has had a few additions, for instance the clock, but it's definitely Lille's gain and Paris's loss. You have a choice now.

End of Walk 1

You have now completed Walk 1.

You could start Walk 2. If that option appeals, follow the instructions "From Flanders Station" on page 10 to reach its start point.

Otherwise, if you want to leave that walk for another day, you can make your way back to the Grand Place as follows:

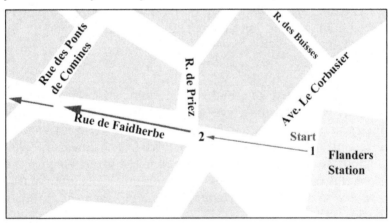

Map 14

Map 14.1 - Stand in front of Flanders station facing away from it. Carefully cross the busy junction in front of you to walk into Rue Faidherbe.

Walk along Rue Faidherbe. You will pass Rue de Priez and Rue de Ponts de Comines on your right.

Rue Faidherbe

Rue Faidherbe used to be a very busy street but the pavements have been widened and the road narrowed to discourage the cars from using it. It's now more pleasant to stroll down.

The street was originally called Rue de La Gare, Station Road. However it was renamed to honour General Faidherbe whose equestrian statue you saw earlier on this walk.

There have been proposals to rename the street again as France tries to bury its colonial past, so when you visit you might find it called something else.

Lille holds a cultural event every three years called Lille 3000. Rue Faidherbe is often decorated as part of that event and in the past it has been home to monumental elephants and towering angels.

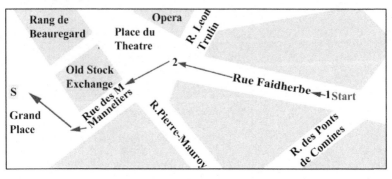

Map 15

Map 15.1 - Continue down Rue Faidherbe and it will take you back to the Place du Theatre.

Map 15.2 - The Grand Place is just one block further along on your left along Rue des Manneliers. Alternatively you could go through the Old Stock Exchange to reach it.

Walk 2 – Lille Old Town

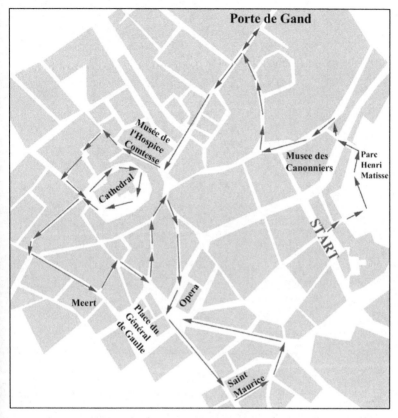

Route Overview

Start this walk in Place Saint Hubert, a little square northeast of Place du Theatre.

If you are in the Place du Theatre, the quickest route to Place Hubert is along Rue Anatole France and Rue de Roubaix. It's about a ten minute walk to get there.

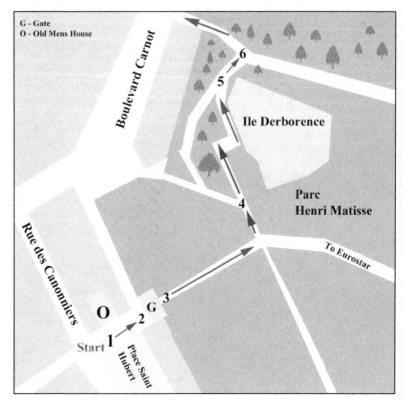

Boulevard Carnot

6

5

Ile Derborence

Parc
Henri Matisse

4

To Eurostar

Rue des Canonniers

O

G 3

2

Start 1

Place Saint Hubert

Map 1

Once there, orientate yourself by keeping Place Saint Hubert on your right-hand side and facing the old Porte de Roubaix gate.

Place Hubert

There is a line of older houses on one side of the square. This little square has recently been renovated, replacing a car park with a pretty cobbled square filled with trees.

On your left at number 4 you will find the Old Men's House.

Maison des Vieux Hommes

Several cities in North Europe had charitable institutions to house and feed destitute elderly men and this was Lille's. It was founded in the early seventeenth century by François Van Hoyqueslot who stated it should house:

> "Three old men, born in Lille,
> at least 55 years old and unable to work".

Other citizens subsequently gave donations to expand it and it was home to Lille's old men until 1797, when its doors were closed and its residents were moved to a much larger Hospice which you will see later.

A large part of The Maison des Vieux Hommes was lost when the Rue des Canonniers was widened. What was left became very rundown but it was restored in the 1980's.

Map 1.1 - Face the Old Men's House. Turn right and walk towards the Porte de Roubaix.

Porte de Roubaix

This gateway is another reminder of Lille's fortifications against invaders. It originally had just one central arch, and the two side arches of the gate were punched through much later to let commuters have easy access into the city by tram.

This gate is not nearly as grand as the Porte de Paris which you saw on Walk 1, but it is actually the most noteworthy. This is where the 35,000 Austrians arrived to invade Lille in 1792, only to find the gate slammed shut.

The Austrians besieged Lille for nine days, and bombarded the city with cannon fire. The town stood firm, led by Mayor Francois Andre and finally the Austrians departed. The mayor and the victory are commemorated by the statue of Déesse in the Grand Place which you saw on walk 1. The Austrians however did do a great deal of damage, including the destruction of the city's main church Saint Etienne which also stood on the Grand Place. It was never rebuilt.

Map 1.2 - Walk through the main archway to enter Parc Henri Matisse.

Turn round to see the gate from the back – it actually looks better from this side. You can see two plaques, one commemorating the gate's construction in 1621 and the other its restoration in 1875.

Map 1.3 - Follow the main path and tram lines through the park for a little way but stop at the first crossroads.

If you were to go straight ahead you would walk towards the Eurostar terminal. Instead turn left.

Map 1.4 - Ignore a path which joins on your left.

The path you are on will go round a walled raised garden on your right. It encloses Derborence Island - which is an experiment.

Derborence Island

It's named after an ancient forest in Switzerland which has survived intact over many thousands of years because it is more or less inaccessible.

This elevated garden has also been made inaccessible and the idea is to see what plants settle without any intervention or contamination by man. Who knows, there could be triffids up there.

Map 1.5 - Another path will join from the left but again ignore it.

Map 1.6 - You will next reach a crossroads amongst the tree. Turn left passing the side of a modern building on your left.

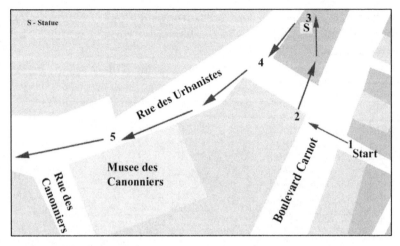

Map 2

Map 2.1 - You will reach Boulevard Carnot. Cross it by the zebra crossing.

Map 2.2 - Then turn right to cross a minor road onto a grassy area with trees. In the middle of the trees is a memorial to Louise de Bettignies.

Louise de Bettignies

She was the woman who is thought to have run the largest spy network of WWI. A soldier humbly kisses her hand.

She was an aristocrat whose family had fallen on hard times, but she was well educated and could speak English, German, and Italian fluently. When Lille was invaded she fled and joined the British Secret Intelligence Service as Alice Dubois, and enlisted eighty other operatives who spied on the German troop movements, munitions locations, and even helped allied soldiers escape back to England.

Sadly she was caught in 1915, and sentenced to fifteen years hard labour by the Germans. She died in 1918 in

Cologne from pneumonia. A book was written about her exploits, called The Queen of Spies, by T. Coulson.

If you look at the bottom of the statue you will see two panels showing a woman being executed. This is not Louise de Bettignies, but Edith Cavell, an English nurse who was executed by the Germans as a spy.

Map 2.3 - Now stand facing the front of the statue. Walk down the busy road on your right-hand side, Rue des Urbanistes.

Map 2.4 - The traffic will mostly swing to the left, but walk straight ahead staying on Rue des Urbanistes. You will reach the Musee des Cannoniers on your left.

Musee des Canonniers

This building was originally a convent but it's now a museum of Lille's artillery. The huge gate has cannons built into its fabric, in place of the more traditional columns. There are also cannonballs perched above the cannons.

King Louis XIV put Lille under siege in1667 when Lille belonged to the Spanish crown. The Canonniers defended their city to the end and after the siege Lille became French. The King had been so impressed by the Canonniers bravery that he ordered that the Canonniers should continue as a military unit. So when the Austrians turned up at the gates in 1792 and again put Lille under siege, the Cannoniers were there once more. They battled to save Lille and never left the walls as they pounded the Austrians with cannon fire. This time the Canonniers were on the winning side.

Above the gate you can see the inscription "'Napoleon 1st Emperor to the Canonniers of Lille'". Napoleon visited Lille with Josephine, and inspected all the fortifications. He approved of Lille and gave this convent to the Canonniers as a reward for saving the city in 1792.

Go through the gate and have a look around the courtyard. You can of course visit the museum if you have time.

The stars of the show are two Gribaeuval cannons which Napoleon gave to the Canonniers – a fact which is proudly inscribed on them. There is only one other surviving cannon of this type in the world, and it's in Paris. Also find the excellent bronze bust of Napoleon I.

Map 2.5 - When you exit, turn left to continue along Rue des Urbanistes passing Rue des Canonniers on your left.

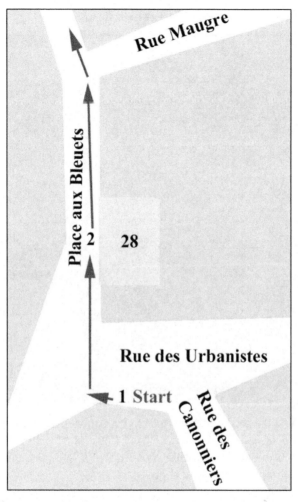

Map 3

Map 3.1 - You will reach a busy junction. Turn right into Place aux Bleuets.

Find the large archway with blue doors on your right at number 28.

Place aux Bleuets Orphanage

In the fifteenth century many children were left orphaned after a series of wars. At first they were simply left to beg to survive, but eventually the church woke up to their plight, rescued them, and housed them on a farm.

A few years later some well-minded citizens contributed to build this orphanage. The orphans were moved here and importantly given the chance to learn a trade. One of the donors stated that the children should be dressed in blue. So when Lille decided to build a square in front of the orphanage, they took its name from the blue uniforms of the orphans – bleuet means blueberry.

The orphanage became a military hospital in the eighteenth century and the children were moved to the Hospice Comtesse which you will see later.

This building is no longer a hospital but it is still used by the army.

Map 3.2 - Continue along Place aux Bleuets passing Rue Maugre on your right. This is a very boring stretch of road but persevere, it gets much better soon.

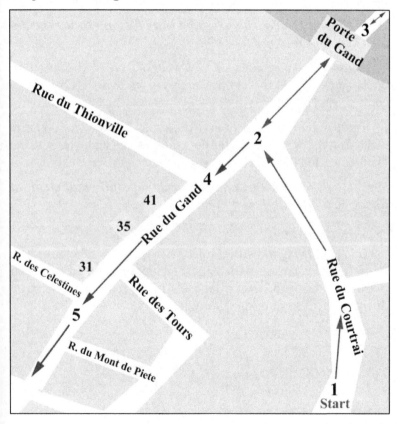

Map 4

Map 4.1 - Walk straight ahead along Rue de Courtrai for about 200 meters to reach a T-junction

Map 4.2 - Turn right to reach Porte de Gand.

Porte de Gand

This was the gate to Ghent and it dates from 1620. The two side archways in the gate were tunnelled to let the trams through in the twentieth century. Upstairs is now an upmarket restaurant.

Walk through the archway and a little beyond to see the old fortifications and moat of Lille.

It gives the best idea of how they survived the Austrian onslaught. Above the central archway you can see the huge coat of arms of Lille.

If you have the energy and the grass is not wet, you can walk down the slope on either side of the gate to see the viaduct leading into the city.

Map 4.3 - Go back through the archway and walk straight ahead to walk into Rue du Gand.

Rue du Gand

This is a lovely old street lined with quaint old houses. The street is also packed with bars and restaurants. It's a great place to eat so do have a look at their menus as you stroll down to see if something takes your fancy.

Map 4.4 - Pass Rue de Thionville and Rue des Célestines on your right.

As you do you will pass numbers 41, 35, and 31, which are all particularly nice old houses.

Map 4.5 - Continue down Rue de Gand passing Rue du Mont de Piete on your left.

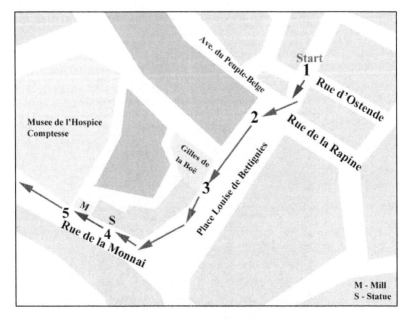

Map 5

Map 5.1 - Pass Rue d'Ostende and Rue de la Rapine on your left. You will reach Place Louise de Bettignies.

Place Louise de Bettignies

This square was named after the Queen of Spies who you read about earlier. It has recently been rescued from being a car park and some potted greenery has been added.

On your right hand side are the long green lawns of Avenue du Peuple Belge. This area is still used by the army and there is a barracks nearby, so perhaps it's not surprising that the Avenue is a red light district - best avoided.

However it's worth noting that the Avenue was originally where one of the two ports sited on the river Duele sat, before the river was rerouted around Lille. The other port lay across the marshes and there was no navigable route between.

Boats were loaded and unloaded at both ports so that the merchandise could be transported to the other side of Lille. At first the goods were simply laboriously carried by men from one port to the other. Later small simple carts were dragged across.

Finally in the eighteenth century someone thought of digging a canal through the marshes, which allowed little boats to do the hard work instead. Later more canals were dug to not only speed transport, but to give the people who lived in Lille an easy way of moving around.

Map 5.2 - Walk down Place Louse de Bettignies.

You will reach a lovely old building on the right-hand side. It has a very ornate façade and houses various little shops.

House of Gilles de la Boë

This is one of Lille's oldest houses. It was built in the seventeenth century for Giles de la Boë who was a spice and cloth merchant.

Giles de la Boë chose an excellent location for his home and business. Not only was it close to the port, it was also just across the road from the old market, Halles Saint Helene, which used to stand at the end of the Avenue du Peuple Belge.

Naturally, as a merchant Giles de la Boë wanted his establishment to attract attention – hence its colourful and ornate façade.

Map 5.3 - Keep the house on your right and continue straight ahead to reach a T-junction.

Turn right into Rue de la Monnaie, the oldest street in the city. Walk halfway along the first block on your right.

Rue de la Monnaie

The street of Money got its name in the seventeenth century when King Louis XIV built a mint here, but sadly the mint has not survived.

On the first floor you will see a pretty little statue of the Virgin Mary and Jesus.

Map 5.4 - At the end of the same block you will reach an odd red brick wall with a doorway and three windows.

The Water Mill

It's all that's left of an ancient watermill said to date from the thirteenth century. As you know this area was very marshy and canals were built to navigate it. The Saint-Pierre canal crossed the street here and in the thirteenth century the Countess of Flanders had a water-mill built.

Look above the doorway and you can see a different date etched, 1649. It's thought the mill burned down after a fire and was later rebuilt.

Look above the left window to see the coat of arms of the Duke of Burgundy sitting over the coat of arms of the House of Flanders. That tells us that the House of Flanders was protected by the powerful Duke of Burgundy.

Sadly another fire hit in the twentieth century and this wall is now all that is left of the water mill.

Map 5.5 - Just past the wall is the Musee de l'Hospice Comtesse. Walk along Rue de Monnaie to reach the large archway which is the entrance.

Musée de l'Hospice Comtesse

This was a 13th century hospital run by nuns and founded by Jeanne of Constantinople, the Countess of Flanders. It is now a museum, and its garden offers a splash of much needed greenery to Lille. The other side of the building used to sit on the riverbank, but of course the river Duele was diverted long ago, and it now faces the Avenue du Peuple Belge.

The museum itself lets you explore the old sick bay, the kitchen with its hundreds of blue and white tiles, the chapel, the former nuns' dormitory, and the lovely courtyard. It's worth hiring the audio guide to understand the full story.

The nuns prepared all the food for themselves and for their patients. They always ate their meals in silence in the refectory, but one of them would stand at a lectern to read from the bible at the same time – just in case the nuns' minds wandered!

The sick bay is a large room where the beds were set into the wall. The patient's privacy was provided only by a curtain. The nuns grew herbs in the garden and made their own medicines. Although their pharmacy and medical knowledge was very limited in what it could do, they did understand the importance of hygiene and diet, so their patients were as well cared for as they could be.

There are wood carvings and tapestries by Guillaume Werniers, a famous Lille weaver, and a very rare collection of musical instruments called the Hel collection. Pierre Hel was a master violin maker who lived and died in Lille in the nineteenth century. He always gave his violins a trademark red varnish to make them stand out.

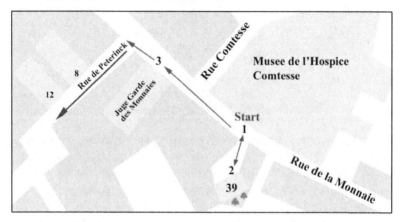

Map 6

Map 6.1 - When you leave the museum, take a few steps into the little alley opposite the museum entrance.

Find the old building on your left-hand side at number 39.

Rue de la Monnaie 39

It dates from the sixteenth century and is partially built of wood. It is thought to be the oldest house in Lille. A new law was introduced in the sixteenth century to stop the construction of any more wooden houses as they were a terrible fire risk. You will get a better view of this half-timbered house later in this walk when you reach the cathedral.

Map 6.2 - Return to Rue de la Monnaie and turn left to reach number 61 on the left. It has an impressive arched entrance.

L'hôtel du Juge Garde des Monnaies

This is the only remnant of the mint which once stood in this street. It was the office of the official who oversaw the staffing and running of the mint. Clearly this was a very important position so the building he was installed in was suitably grand.

Map 6.3 - Take the next left into Rue de Pétérinck and continue to Number 8 on your right.

Rue de Pétérinck

In medieval times a little stream ran down the middle of the street. It is now a pleasant cobbled street and has several nice restaurants worth taking note of.

Long ago however this was a very different type of neighbourhood. Notice the little doors at the bottom of the buildings – those gave light and air to the cellars where whole families lived and worked as weavers in dire poverty.

By the early nineteenth century, linen weaving was one of Lille's most important businesses. However all the wealth generated was still based on the labour of poor weaving families working in the cellars of streets like this.

When Victor Hugo visited Lille he was shown around cellars like these. He was appalled at the conditions he found people living in and he wrote a powerful speech called

"Destroy misery; the cellars of Lille"

Unfortunately he never gave it because of the instability of French politics at the time.

When industrialisation arrived the weaving industry petered out, and this neighbourhood became even poorer and a dangerous place to linger. Even as late as the 1970's, this was one of the poorest and most dilapidated areas in Lille. A decision was taken to renovate the buildings, so the residents were moved out to other parts of Lille. Their old homes were restored and are now ironically in one of the most sought after places to live in Lille!

The carving above the door of number 8 is called the "The Golden Well" and it is designated as a listed building.

A little further along at number 12 is a sculpture of Mary and Jesus, sitting above what is at the time of writing a wine bar.

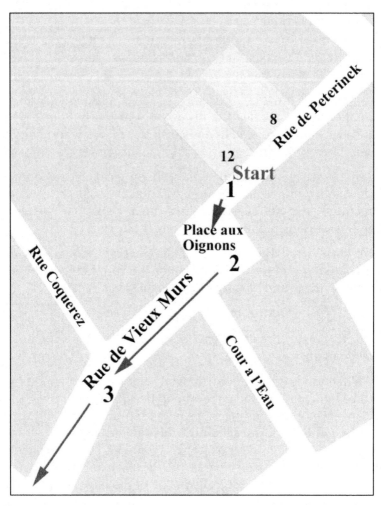

Map 7

Map 7.1 – Continue along Rue du Peterinck to reach a little square called Place aux Oignons – Onion square.

Onion Square

The square actually gets its name from the word "donjon" which means "keep" and has nothing to do with onions. The old fortress belonging to the Count of Flanders stood near here but nothing of it remains except the name.

The crumbling buildings which stood here were also renovated in the 1970's making it one of the nicest little corners in Lille. If you pass through the square at the weekend there are often some stalls selling knick-knacks.

Map 7.2 - Leave the square by Rue des Vieux Murs to continue in the same direction.

Map 7.3 - Pass Rue Coquourez on your right and continue to reach a T junction with Rue des Trois Mollettes.

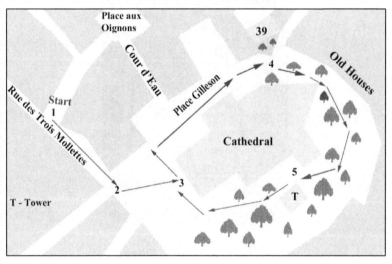

Map 8

Map 8.1 - Turn left to reach the square the cathedral lies on.

Rue des Trois Mollettes

This is another of Lille's lovely old cobbled streets. If you like beer you might want to return to this street later to investigate Le Capsule, which lies at number 25 and is said to be one of the best beer bars in France.

Map 8.2 – Turn left as you enter the square to approach the cathedral.

Notre-Dame de la Treille Cathedral

This is a cathedral you will either love or hate.

In the twelfth century an old church in Lille had a statue of the Virgin Mary. It was protected by a trellis - hence the name "treille". The statue had several miracles attributed to it so it was decided to build this cathedral to house it.

The cathedral started life in 1854 and architects were invited to submit their ideas. The first two winning designs were discarded when the authorities discovered that the architects were protestant – the third design was by a catholic and accepted.

The church did not actually get completed until the 1990s as they ran out of money. It was originally designed to have two towers but they didn't get built. So instead they decided to erect a temporary smaller brick tower. It took them just one month to build it and it is still there today. If you face the front of the Cathedral the tower stands to the right, only meters away from the Cathedral itself. It holds the cathedrals 41 bells.

If you manage to visit on Sunday near a service time, you will be treated to an enthusiastic cascade of bells which is out of all proportion to the size of the tower!

Sadly, the statue of Mary which the cathedral was built to house was pinched in the 1950's and has never been found.

The Door

Do take a few minutes to look closely at the main door of the cathedral. It is full in little intricate carvings.

Inside

The cathedral is very austere from the outside; in fact the steel network around the central section might make you think that the scaffolding is still up. However venture in on a sunny day and see the surprising orange pink glow through the translucent veil of marble.

It also has a very modern rose stained glass window which apparently represents the death of Jesus and the resurrection. However its meaning is not clear to most people – including me; the image has unusual items like UFOs, cosmonauts, and "E=mc2".

Walk around the church to see both the marble wall and the rose window with the light streaming in.

There are several chapels to explore, all decorated with beautiful stained glass windows.

La Sainte Chapelle

At the far end of the church is the beautiful and colourful La Sainte Chapelle.

The altar holds a statue of Notre Dame de la Treille which was created to replace the original ancient statue which was stolen in 1959.

Around you the walls are covered in mosaics depicting famous scenes and female characters from the Old Testament. Spot Noah's ark and Eve!

Make your way outside again

The square around the Cathedral is very popular at the weekend. There are several cafes and if you are here on a sunny day it's a very pleasant place to just relax and watch the locals do the same.

Round the Cathedral

Map 8.3 - Face the front of the Cathedral and go down its left-hand side which is called Place Gilleson.

As you do, you will pass a large white building with a stepped entrance on your left. Just beyond that you will find some trees, and behind them stands the oldest house in Lille which you saw earlier on this walk. You can see much more of the wooden timbers from this side.

Map 8.4 - Continue walking around the cathedral.

You will see the charming colourful old houses on your left-hand side. Some of them still have little bridges which crossed the old canal which ran along here but which is now gone.

Map 8.5 - You will eventually reach the bell-tower. Continue to return to the front of the Cathedral.

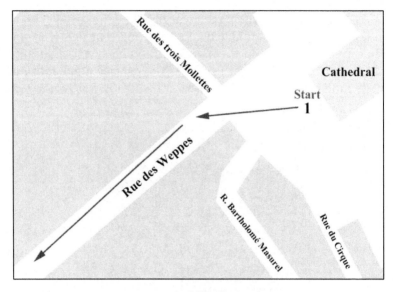

Map 9

Map 9.1 – Stand at the Cathedral door facing away from the Cathedral. Cross the square diagonally right and walk down Rue de Weppes.

Rue de Weppes

This old street used to be the Pont-de-Weppes canal until the river Deûle was diverted beyond the boundaries of Lille and the canals were covered over.

This was a very unhygienic stretch of water and caused many epidemics – which was one of the main reasons the waterways were diverted away from Lille.

The Pont-de-Weppes canal was the last to be covered over, only in the 1930s. Its old route is now a very pleasant walk.

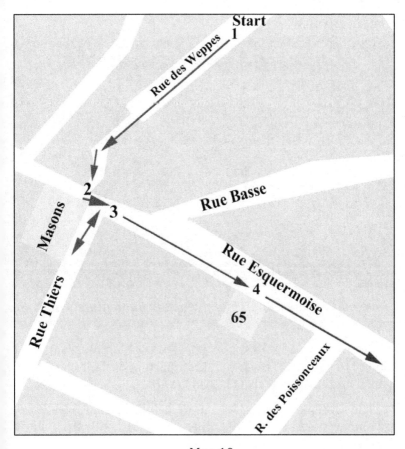

Map 10

Map 10.1 - Walk to the end of the street where it will narrow and become a path, and finally a short tunnel.

You will see empty ditches on either side of the pathway – all that remains of the canal. At the end of the path cross one of the few surviving bridges over the waterway, although there is of course no sign of any water.

Map 10.2 – You will reach a T junction with Rue Esquermoise. Turn left but just take a few steps.

Freemansons

Have a look down Rue Thiers which is immediately on your right.

You will see a large sphinx above a door on the right hand side of the street. This is the headquarters of the Freemasons which is still very much a force in France.

The Sphinx is said to be the Guardian of Mysteries, presumably that includes the meaning of the funny handshakes freemasons are so fond of.

Walking along Rue Esquermoise

Map 10.3 - Continue along Rue Esquermoise passing Rue Basse on your left. Pause at number 65 on your right.

You will see two lovely statues holding up the balcony at number 65.

Map 10.4 – Continue along Rue Esquermoise, passing Rue des Poissonceaux on your right.

It translates as "Fish Water", and the old Canal de Poissonceaux ran just behind it. It was covered over in the nineteenth century, and you may have already read about it if you have done Walk 1.

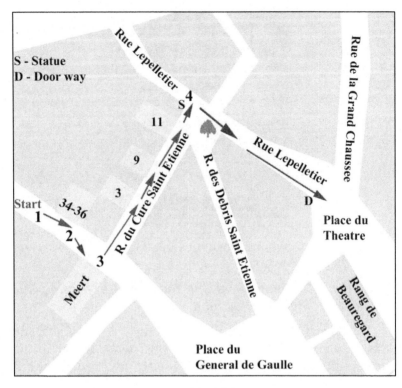

Map 11

Map 11.1 - Further along you will find numbers 34 and 36 on your left.

They have very pretty facades and are classified as historic monuments. Around them are other buildings which have handsome iron balconies.

Map 11.2 - Continue to number 27 on your right hand side where you will find Meert.

Meert

This is a beautiful patisserie, chocolatier and teashop – they have fifty types of tea to choose from!

It dates from 1761 and some say it's the oldest patisserie in the world. Its current appearance is down to owner Monsieur Rollez who had the original building beautifully renovated in 1839 – look up to the wrought iron balcony to see the "R" for Rollez in the ironwork. The façade was the work of architect Benvignat and sculptor Huidiez, and they were obviously proud of the result as their names appear at the bottom of the two doors.

Inside it is full of sparkling chandeliers, gilded wood, and mirrors. Look at the front of the serving counters to see the "R" for Rollez again.

Rollez specialised in ice-cream, but Monsieur Meert from Belgium took over in 1849 and turned his attention to patisserie. All the delicious pastries are made on-site, and they use only the very best ingredients, including vanilla from Madagascar. It was the vanilla waffles or "guafres" which first brought fame to Meert's establishment, so now each guafre has "Meert" stamped on it.

Charles de Gaulle loved to visit, and his favourite indulgence was indeed a guafre. They are very, very sweet, but there are many other delights to try. Meert expanded and there are now branches in many of Europe's cities, but this is where it all started.

If you browse around the shop you will find the tea selection includes one called Buffalo Bill. William Cody brought his Wild West show to Lille in 1905, and ordered 80 kilos of tea from Meert. So Meert celebrated that event with a blend of tea named after the showman. If you have time, stop in the lovely upstairs tearoom and indulge yourself.

Map 11.3 - When you leave Meert, cross the road to enter Rue du Cure Saint Etienne.

Rue du Cure Saint-Étienne

There is an interesting fromagerie at number 3 called Philippe Olivier. It has been around since 1903. It specialises in unusual cheeses, so have a look in the window - you might see a Mont des Cats which comes from the Trappist monasteries, or a Maroilles which was first made by monks in 962.

Numbers 9 and 11 are also listed as historical monuments due to their ornate upper floors. On number 9 on the second floor you will see another example of the hugging and snubbing angels.

At the end of Rue du Cure Saint-Étienne and on your left hand side you will find Rue Lepelletier (Furrier Street).

Abraham

Look up at the building on that corner and you will see a carving of the date 1716 in Rue du Cure Saint-Étienne.

Just round the corner in Rue Lepelletier you will see the Sacrifice of Abraham with the angel arriving just in time to stop Abraham killing his son.

Map 11.4 - Now orientate yourself by standing in Rue Lepelletier, with the Sacrifice of Abraham on your right-hand side.

You will see a tree in front of you. Behind the tree, you will see that the road forks. Go down the left-hand side of the tree, staying on Rue Lepelletier.

Walk towards the Place du Theatre – you can see the clock tower in the distance.

The Furrier

Right at the end of Rue Lepelletier and on your right-hand side you will find a very ancient archway, now incorporated into a shop.

It is dated 1677 at the top, and above the entrance are some very indistinct carvings. The experts tell us that the carvings are of a lamb and a deer which were used in the fur trade – this doorway was the entrance to a furrier's shop long ago.

If you are weary, you can finish this walk in Place du Theatre which Rue Lepelletier runs into.

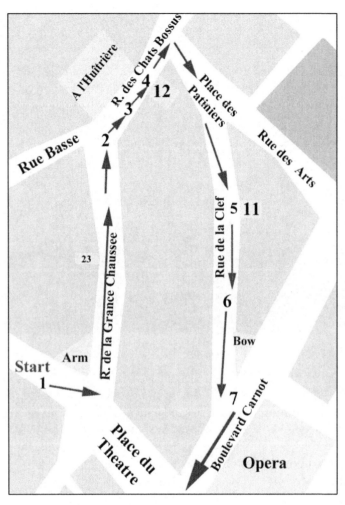

Map 12

Map 12.1 - If on the other hand you are ready for a few more cobbled streets, follow the direction pointed to by the golden arm you can see high on the building on your left.

It's at the corner of Rue Lepelletier and Rue de la Grande Chaussee.

The golden arm belonged to a glove-maker's shop which stood here long ago. Enter Rue de la Grande Chaussee.

This street is very old – it is mentioned in a charter from 1066 as running from the Grand Place to where the cathedral stands today. It was once lined with wooden houses, but they fell victim to a fire in the sixteenth century. It was that fire which convinced Lille's rulers to ban the use of wood in house building.

The street is full of lovely iron balconies, so look up to the first floor as you stroll down. Pause at number 23 – it's on your left just as the road starts to gently curve left. You will see a little ship carved into one of the iron balconies. It's a reminder that Lille traded by the waterways long ago.

Map 12.2 - You will reach a T junction with Rue de Chats Bossus on your right and Rue Basse on your left.

Turn right into Rue Chat Bossus (street of the Hunchbacked Cats).

A l'Huîtrière,

At number 3 you will find a shop which was once "A l'Huîtrière", one of Lille's most famous seafood establishments.

The owners invested in a colourful Art Deco exterior – bright fish and marine plants fill the facade. Sadly the shop closed its doors some years ago, and Lille has been waiting to see who would take it over.

It's a listed building now so the Art Deco façade will survive, but who knows what will be on sale. Perhaps when you visit you can find out.

Map 12.3 - Face A l'Huîtrière and turn right along Rue Chat Bossus to reach number 12 on your right.

Here you will find a hunchbacked cat looking ready to pounce on you.

The Hunchbacked Cat

There are two theories as to where this street's odd name comes from.

The first is that it's derived from the old word "caboche" which meant head, and referred to the skulls of animals which were piled up here by the tanners who worked in this street.

The other is that it refers to an old cabaret which stood here and had a hunchbacked cat on its sign – which is a more appealing explanation.

114

Map 12.4 - Continue along the street and turn right into Place des Patiniers.

You will reach a fork in the road. Take the narrow right-hand street, Rue de la Clef.

Rue de la Clef

This is one of the oldest streets in Lille and it gets its current name from a hotel which stood here in the eighteenth century, l'Hotel de la Clef". Just a few decades ago tourists would not venture down this street as it was a red light district.

Then it went through two transformations, firstly a youth culture took over and start-up designers, games shops, and record stores moved in. It became gentrified and is now home to more well-known luxury shops, but it still has some unusual establishments.

Map 12.5 - Find the Cirque Marionnettes dans Cinema at number 34 on the left-hand side.

Cirque Marionnettes dans Cinema

It's easy to spot with a rather ancient mask hanging outside the shop.

It's a specialised bookshop selling performing arts books, and occasionally the owners organise a show outside the shop to encourage people to venture inside. So you may find something interesting going on as you pass.

Map 12.6 – Rue de la Clef runs into Boulevard Carnot. When it does, turn round to see a wonderfully narrow building at the junction.

The Bow

This building is nicknamed The Bow because it looks like the bow of a ship. It was the first building of a much larger planned redevelopment of this street which never got any further.

Map 12.7 - Continue along Boulevard Carnot and it will take you back to Place du Theatre.

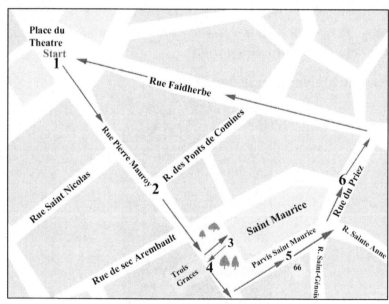

Map 13

Map 13.1 - Now stand just in front of the Old Stock Exchange and face the Opera. Turn right and leave by Rue Pierre Mauroy

Rue Pierre Mauroy

The road was called Rue de Paris until a few years ago, but was then renamed to honour the mayor of Lille who became the Prime Minister of France for three years during the presidency of Mitterrand.

Map 13.2 Pass Rue des Ponts de Comines on your left. Walk towards the trees which you can see a few blocks ahead of you.

On your left you will find the church of Saint Maurice.

Saint Maurice

Saint Maurice was a Christian from Egypt, who was also the leader of the Theban Legion of the Roman Army. On a campaign in Switzerland, the legion was ordered to clear the Saint Bernard Pass. They were also commanded to massacre a Swiss village at the same time to terrify the locals. The Christians in the army refused so the Emperor had Maurice and the other uncooperative Christians executed. That Swiss village is now known as Saint-Maurice-en-Valais.

This church was started in the fourteenth century and is actually much more Flemish in style than French. Thanks to the constant invasions and battles which Lille had to endure, it took more than four hundred years to actually complete. However, stand at the front and you will agree it was worth the wait. The reason it has such a wide front, is that you are standing on what was once marshy ground, so the church was spread out to distribute the weight.

The church has been sandblasted back to its original pristine colour.

Go inside and pick up the little leaflet and guide. It will show you the little painting of Saint Maurice himself which is the oldest painting in the church, so see if you can find it.

If you stand right in the centre of the church you will be in the oldest section which was built in the fourteenth century. As you walk towards either the front or the rear door, you will pass through the extensions added across the centuries.

Some of the stained glass windows were hit during bombing raids in World War I and II, and have been replaced with very colourful modern glass.

WW I Memorial

There is also a memorial to the men of the British Empire who lost their lives in World War I.

It is one of a series of memorials which were placed in 28 cathedrals and churches of towns of France and Belgium where the British troops had been stationed. If you visit any of those locations you will find an almost identical memorial plaque to this one. The memorial tablet was used as a model and installed all over the British Empire. The words of the memorial which refer to the "million dead" were written by Rudyard Kipling.

Also worth a look are the wonderfully carved pulpit and its stairway.

Map 13.3 - Exit the church via the front door and look up at number 74 Rue de Paris which is just opposite.

Maison des Trois Grâces

This lovely old building is called the Maison des Trois Grâces.

Decorating the first floor are three Greek goddesses, Juno with an eagle, Minerva wearing her helmet, and Venus with Cupid.

Map 13.4 - Turn left and then left again into Parvis Saint-Maurice.

Just before you reach a junction with Rue Saint-Génois, you will find an old building housing an artisan baker at number 66.

Maison du Renard

The building is known as the "Maison du Renard", the house of the fox, and if you look up you will see a fox on the second floor above a window.

Map 13.5 - Face the Maison du Renard and turn left. Pass Rue Saint-Génois and Rue Sainte Anne on your right. Walk along Rue du Priez to reach the end of the church.

From Rue du Priez you get the best view of the back of the church.

Map 13.6 – From Rue du Prieze walk straight ahead to reach a T-junction with Rue Faidherbe.

Turn left into Rue Faidherbe which will take you back to Place du Theatre and the end of the walk.

Did you enjoy these walks?

I do hope you found these walks both fun and interesting, and I would love feedback, so please review this book

You could also drop me a line on my amazon web page.

Printed in Great Britain
by Amazon

16918670R00071